The Train to Spain

Mary Elizabeth Salzmann

Consulting Editor, Diane Craig, M.A./Reading Specialist

ABDO
Publishing Company

Published by ABDO Publishing Company, 4940 Viking Drive, Edina, Minnesota 55435.

Printed in the United States.

Credits
Edited by: Pam Price
Curriculum Coordinator: Nancy Tuminelly
Cover and Interior Design and Production: Mighty Media
Photo Credits: AbleStock, Hemera, Photodisc

Library of Congress Cataloging-in-Publication Data

Salzmann, Mary Elizabeth, 1968-
    The train to Spain / Mary Elizabeth Salzmann.
        p. cm. -- (First rhymes)
    Includes index.
    ISBN 1-59679-541-7 (hardcover)
    ISBN 1-59679-542-5 (paperback)
        1. English language--Rhyme--Juvenile literature. I. Title. II. Series.
    PE1517.S3596 2005
    808.1--dc22
                                                                    2005048809

SandCastle™ books are created by a professional team of educators, reading specialists, and content developers around five essential components that include phonemic awareness, phonics, vocabulary, text comprehension, and fluency. All books are written, reviewed, and leveled for guided reading and early intervention reading, and designed for use in shared, guided, and independent reading and writing activities to support a balanced approach to literacy instruction.

Let Us Know

After reading the book, SandCastle would like you to tell us your stories about reading. What is your favorite page? Was there something hard that you needed help with? Share the ups and downs of learning to read. We want to hear from you! To get posted on the ABDO Publishing Company Web site, send us e-mail at:

sandcastle@abdopub.com

SandCastle Level: Beginning

grain

plain

rain

Spain

train

Here is some .

4

This is a .

See the .

This is .

Here is a .

This grain is wheat.

The plain is flat.

The rain is wet.

This country is Spain.

The train goes fast.

The Train to Spain

Farmer Dwain
lives on a flat plain.

Farmer Dwain
grows grain
on the plain.

Farmer Dwain
takes the grain
across the plain
on a train.

20

Farmer Dwain
takes the train of grain
from the plain
all the way to Spain.

When Farmer Dwain
and his train of grain
from the plain
get to Spain,
it starts to rain.

About SandCastle™

A professional team of educators, reading specialists, and content developers created the SandCastle™ series to support young readers as they develop reading skills and strategies and increase their general knowledge. The SandCastle™ series has four levels that correspond to early literacy development in young children. The levels are provided to help teachers and parents select the appropriate books for young readers.

Emerging Readers
(no flags)

Beginning Readers
(1 flag)

Transitional Readers
(2 flags)

Fluent Readers
(3 flags)

These levels are meant only as a guide. All levels are subject to change.

ABDO
Publishing Company

To see a complete list of SandCastle™ books and other nonfiction titles from ABDO Publishing Company, visit **www.abdopub.com** or contact us at:
4940 Viking Drive, Edina, Minnesota 55435 • 1-800-800-1312 • fax: 1-952-831-1632